Adult Coloring for Relaxation

By Spring's Designs

April 2021

Single paged for no bleed-through.

Be Inspired.

Be Creative.

Be unique.

DESPITE THE WEATHER, LIVE LIKE IT'S ALWAYS SPRING.

NEVER
give
UP

Spring Butterflies

If you want
a rainbow,
you have to
put up with a
little rain.

Believe in yourself.

Be Bold

Be Brave

SEIZE
THE
DAY

In a field
full of daisies,
be a rose.

live
your
dream.

reach
for
the
stars!

Just breathe...

Be Inspired.

Be Creative.

Be Unique.